Best-Loved Lavender Recipes

Nancy Baggett

Copyright © 2023 by Nancy Baggett

All rights reserved.

No part of this book may be reproduced in any form without written permission from Nancy Baggett.

Copies of this book are available for purchase at:
www.nancyslavenderplace.com

Published in 2023 by
Kitchenlane Productions
P.O. Box 1453 Columbia, MD 21044

Photography: Nancy Baggett

Cover and Interior Design and Production: Cathy Gibbons Reedy

Printed in China

Contents

Cooking with Lavender, 5
Beverages & Snacks, 8
Soups, Mains & Sides, 22
Desserts & Baked Goods, 42
Pantry & Refrigerator Staples, 64

Cooking with Lavender

Culinary lavender is an easy way to add wonderful flavor and fragrance to dishes. But start by understanding that not all lavenders taste good or are suitable for cooking. You need to look for a product labeled *culinary lavender*, or "English" lavender, or *Lavandula angustifolia*, aka "true" lavender. True lavenders, technically known as angustifolias, have a chameleon-like spicy, citrusy, piney character that can magically brighten up all sorts of both savory and sweet ingredients.

Ironically, except for one variety called 'Provence,' most "French" lavenders, aka lavandin or x *intermedia* lavenders, are grown for cosmetics use. They smell great in soaps and such but are too pungent and camphorous for cooking. Varieties labeled "Spanish" or *stoechas* lavenders—which you can identify by their little plumes rising from barrel-shaped bloom heads—are usually bitter tasting and not suitable for cooking either.

Since culinary lavender is a minor product in the French lavender industry, for the freshest, best-quality culinary lavender seek out North American–grown buds or bunches from small, family-run lavender farms. Buy from them online or at farmers' markets, or for an unforgettable treat, purchase your lavender during a visit to a farm when the fields are in bloom. Ask for their favorite culinary lavender, and if you buy a fresh bunch, hang it upside-down at home to dry and pluck off the blooms to cook with as you need them.

Cooking Tips

Lavender is an unusual herb in that the flowers, commonly called buds, are the edible parts, not the leaves. The buds are actually made up of two parts, little tubes called calyxes and tiny "bloomlets" called corollas on top. The fresh bloomlets are tender and mild and can be plucked off and strewn over cold dishes for a lovely garnish (see p. 39); they fade and drop off as the buds dry. The remaining tube-shaped parts of the buds have most of the plant's oil sacs, and these contribute much of the prized flavor and aroma. The buds are more potent and concentrated once dried, so be a little more generous if cooking with fresh buds.

- Avoid lengthy boiling of lavender or long exposure to high heat; this turns its flavor harsh.

- Lavender is a potent, assertive herb, so if you're a newbie use a light hand. (Some recipes suggest a quantity range, such as 1 to 1 1/2 teaspoons to guide you.)

- Never cook with lavender essential oil, even culinary lavender oil; it is too potent to consume, plus the distillation process often makes it taste unpleasant.

- Try subbing culinary lavender in recipes calling for rosemary or thyme, or use it along with them. It has a somewhat similar scent and pungency, yet is a nice change of pace.

- Many recipes call for steeping lavender buds in water, then straining them out, or grinding them with sugar and sifting out any remaining bits. So have on hand a very fine mesh sieve, or better yet, small and large ones.

- Like most herbs, lavender gets stale with long storage. If your supply smells musty-dusty, it's time to restock.

- Culinary lavenders can be white, pale pink, blue to deep purple, and *all can be equally tasty*. Just be sure you're cooking with *culinary* lavender buds.

BEVERAGES & SNACKS

BEVERAGES & SNACKS

Easy Lavender Pink Lemonade

This lovely—and very popular—lavender thirst-quencher starts with a quart of ready-to-serve pink lemonade from the supermarket dairy case. It's jazzed up not only with lavender but with some fresh lemon juice and slices. If you use regular lemonade, the lavender will give it a slight pinkish tinge, but not the vivid color shown in the photo here.

TIP: Lemon slices help boost the cheerful look and fresh, citrusy taste of purchased lemonade, but remove them from the serving pitcher after a half hour or so. While the yellow zest parts lend welcome flavor, the white pith will gradually turn the lemonade bitter.

- -

1 quart ready-to-use dairy case pink lemonade, well chilled	2 medium-sized well-washed lemons
1 tablespoon dried culinary lavender buds	2 to 3 cups ice, plus more for serving
	Fresh or dried, lavender sprigs for garnish, optional

Stir together 1/4 cup of the lemonade and the lavender buds in a 2-cup microwave-safe glass measure. Microwave on full power for 45 seconds. Stop and stir, then microwave on 50 percent power 1 minute longer. To avoid any chance of a boil-over, let stand to steep and cool in the microwave oven for 5 to 10 minutes. (Steep longer for more pronounced lavender flavor.)

Meanwhile, put the rest of the lemonade in a large serving pitcher. Cut the lemons into slices, discarding seeds. Strain the steeped lavender lemonade liquid through a fine mesh sieve into the pitcher, pressing down firmly to force through as much liquid as possible. Add 5 or 6 lemon slices and stir well. Then add ice to the pitcher. Pour the lemonade over ice-filled glasses, garnishing the servings with fresh lemon slices and lavender sprigs, as desired.

BEVERAGES & SNACKS

Microwave Mug of Lavender Hot Chocolate

I start nearly every day with this quick, delish mug of hot chocolate. No, hot cocoa and hot chocolate *are not* the same. Hot chocolate is prepared using chocolate, not cocoa powder. This recipe conveniently calls for the same semisweet or bittersweet chocolate morsels you likely have stashed in the cupboard to bake chocolate chip cookies. Or substitute part of a chopped up bar of eating chocolate.

I like bittersweet morsels or bars containing 60 to 70% cacao for this recipe. The higher cacao percentage delivers robust chocolate flavor and is not too sweet. Although any lavender syrup will do for sweetening, try the Lavender-Ginger Syrup version (p. 68), for a unique and particularly delectable hot chocolate.

TIP: The only little trick is to follow the directions and stir just a little milk into the chocolate at the start: Chocolate is finicky and blends best if stirred together with a small amount of hot liquid first.

- 1/3 cup chocolate morsels or chopped chocolate eating bar
- 1 1/2 cups whole or 2% fat milk, or unsweetened almond milk, divided
- 1 to 2 tablespoons lavender syrup (p. 65), gourmet lavender-fruit syrup (p. 66), or lavender-ginger syrup (p. 68) to taste
- Mini- marshmallows or sweetened whipped cream for garnish, optional

Put the morsels or chopped chocolate in a 2-cup or larger microwave-safe mug. Add about 1/4 cup milk (no need to measure). Microwave on full power for 1 minute. Stir well, continuing until the chocolate melts and the mixture becomes smoother; this may take a minute or two. Stir in the remaining milk.

Microwave on full power for 1 1/2 minutes. Let the mixture stand in the microwave to cool for 1 minute. If it's still very hot, remove it using a kitchen mitt or potholder. Stir in the lavender syrup to taste. If necessary, reheat the hot chocolate on full power for 30 seconds, or until piping hot. Top the mug with some mini- marshmallows or a dollop of whipped cream and serve. Makes a single 1 1/2-cup serving.

BEVERAGES & SNACKS

BEVERAGES & SNACKS

BEVERAGES & SNACKS

Lavender-Spice Mulled Apple Cider

I love the seasoning combo in this super-fragrant and full-bodied apple cider. I call for whole spices because they taste fresher and don't leave residue in the cider. The cider will disappear quickly when served at any fall or winter event. It's quite convenient to serve it in a crockpot.

TIP: Cardamom seeds (sometimes still in their pods) add great flavor, but they are pricey and hard to find, so omit them if you must.

- 2 quarts good-quality sweet (not hard) apple cider
- 2 to 3 teaspoons packed light or dark brown sugar, optional
- 4 or 5 nickel-sized thin slices peeled fresh gingerroot
- 1 2-to-3 teaspoons dried culinary lavender buds
- 1 2-to-3-inch cinnamon stick, broken in half or thirds
- 1 1/2-inch piece vanilla bean, coarsely chopped or broken into small pieces or 1/2 teaspoon vanilla extract
- 1 teaspoon whole allspice berries, slightly crushed
- 1/2 teaspoon green cardamom seeds, slightly crushed, optional
- 4 whole cloves, slightly crushed
  Small crab apples and culinary lavender sprigs for garnish, optional

In a 4-quart or similar stainless-steel, enameled or other nonreactive saucepan, stir together the cider, sugar (if using), gingerroot, lavender, cinnamon, vanilla, allspice, cardamom (if using), and cloves. Heat over medium-high heat just to a simmer, then adjust the heat so the mixture barely simmers, uncovered, for at least 30 minutes and up to 1 hour. If using immediately, strain the cider through a very fine mesh sieve and serve, garnished with small crab apples or orange slices, and lavender sprigs, if desired.

Alternatively for convenience or even more flavorful cider, let cool, then refrigerate, covered, up to 3 days. Then strain out the spices using a fine mesh sieve. Reheat the mulled cider until piping not but not boiling and serve. Makes about 6 8-ounce servings, or 1 1/2 quarts (due to the evaporation during simmering).

BEVERAGES & SNACKS

BEVERAGES & SNACKS

Lavender Peach Berry Smoothie

If you like smoothies you really should try this recipe—for breakfast, lunch, or as a gratifying snack. The fruit, lavender, and berry flavor blend is outstanding. To keep preparations super-quick always have a bag of ready-to-use frozen peach slices stashed in the freezer and a bottle of lavender syrup and pomegranate juice in the refrigerator.

• •

1	cup peeled fresh or frozen (partially thawed) peach slices	1/3	cup bottled pomegranate juice
1	5.3 ounce carton full-fat or low-fat Greek-style strawberry or blueberry yogurt	2-to-3	tablespoons lavender syrup (p. 65) or gourmet lavender-fruit syrup (p. 66)

Combine the peaches, yogurt, pomegranate juice, and lavender syrup in a food processor or blender. Process or blend for several minutes, stopping and scraping down the sides several times until the peaches are smoothly pureed. (A processor will take longer, and the results will not be as smooth.) Pour into a glass and serve. Makes a 1 1/2-cup serving.

BEVERAGES & SNACKS

Lavender-Apple Spice Tea

Lavender-apple spice tea is a simple, truly delightful way to answer the question, "I have some culinary lavender buds, what can I do with them?" Readied quickly in a microwave oven, the recipe makes a smallish pot of tea (2 cups). But you can double or triple it, if desired.

TIP: Let the tea cool a bit and serve over ice for a pleasant, warm-weather thirst quencher.

1	cup apple juice	1	heaping teaspoon dried culinary lavender buds
1	chai-flavored (regular or decaf) commercial tea bag		Clover or other mild honey, or other preferred sweetener, to taste

Combine 1 cup water, the apple juice, tea bag, and lavender buds in a microwave-safe teapot, or substitute a 4-cup glass measure. If the pot has a strainer insert, put the lavender in the insert; otherwise just stir it into the water. In a microwave on full power, heat the tea just until it barely comes to a boil, 2 to 4 minutes depending on your microwave; watch carefully after 2 minutes and immediately stop when you see any signs of boiling. To avoid any chance of a boil-over, let the tea stand in the microwave 4 minutes to steep and cool slightly. Then remove the strainer inset and pour the tea into cups. If lacking an insert, pour the tea through a fine mesh sieve into cups to strain out the lavender first. Stir in honey to taste. Makes two 1-cup servings.

BEVERAGES & SNACKS

BEVERAGES & SNACKS

BEVERAGES & SNACKS

Lavender Pineapple-Orange Mimosas (or Mocktails) for a Crowd

Many people have heard that lavender pairs well with lemon. But did you know it is particularly delectable with pineapple? One sip and you will notice that these mimosas are special—the intermingling of the lavender, a little honey, and pineapple with the orange juice just creates a subtle but memorable flavor.

TIP: If you like, substitute chilled ginger ale for the wine to create refreshing, very festive mocktails.

- -

- 2 teaspoons dried culinary lavender buds
- 2 to 3 tablespoons clover or orange blossom honey, to taste
- 2 cups chilled bottled pineapple juice
- 2 cups chilled bottled orange juice, preferably pulp-free
- Small fresh pineapple tidbits, mini orange wedges on swizzle sticks and dried lavender sprigs for garnish, optional
- 1 750 ml bottle well-chilled Prosecco or other sparkling or still fruity white wine

Combine 1/4 cup water and the lavender buds in a 2-cup or larger glass measure. Heat in a microwave oven on 100 percent power for 1 1/2 minutes. Let stand to steep and cool in the microwave for 3 minutes. Stir in the honey until dissolved; set aside until cooled. Use immediately, or cover and refrigerate up to 24 hours before serving.

At serving time, strain the lavender-honey mixture through a fine sieve into a serving pitcher, pressing down to force through as much liquid as possible. Thoroughly stir the pineapple and orange juices into the pitcher. Divide among 6 to 8 stemmed glasses or other wine glasses. Garnish the glasses with some pineapple and orange pieces on swizzle sticks and some lavender sprigs, if desired. Add about 1/2 cup wine or amount desired to each glass, and serve immediately. Makes 6 to 8 servings.

BEVERAGES & SNACKS

Chipotle Honey-Roasted Nuts with Lavender and Rosemary

These have a little kick from chipotle and make a tempting, not-too-sweet treat or snack. Most people find their intriguing salty-hot-sweet-herbal flavor and pleasing crunchy-munchiness hard to resist.

TIP: The recipe yields 3/4 pound of roasted nuts. But if you use two roasting pans, it's a simple matter to prepare a double batch. (Which will likely disappear quickly!)

- -

1/3	cup clover honey or other mild honey	3	cups (about 12 ounces) raw pecan or walnut halves, or skinned whole hazelnuts or almonds
1	tablespoon safflower, sunflower, or other neutral-flavored oil	1/4	to 1/2 teaspoon coarse sea salt, to taste, plus more for garnish if desired
2	teaspoons *each* dried culinary lavender buds and chopped dried rosemary leaves	3	to 4 teaspoons red, purple, or clear coarse sparkling crystal sugar for garnish, optional
1/4	to 3/4 teaspoon chipotle chile powder, to taste		

Preheat the oven to 325 degrees F. Generously spray a large rimmed baking sheet with nonstick coating. Thoroughly stir together the honey, oil, lavender, rosemary, and chipotle powder in a 2-cup heat proof glass measure. Watching carefully, microwave on 100 percent power for 40 to 50 seconds; stop microwaving when the honey begins to bubble up. Let stand in the microwave for 10 to 15 minutes.

Strain the honey mixture through a fine sieve into a large bowl. Immediately thoroughly stir in the nuts and salt; completely coat with the honey. Spread out the nuts and honey on the sheet. Roast (middle rack) for 10 minutes, then stir well. Roast for 8 to 10 minutes longer, continuing until the nuts are well browned. If necessary, stir and then roast the nuts for 5 minutes longer. If desired, garnish with a little more coarse crystal salt and chipotle powder for flavor, and coarse crystal sugar for sparkle, crunch and color. Stir and let the nuts stand to completely cool; then separate with forks. Store airtight and refrigerated for up to a month. Serve at room temperature. Makes a generous 3 cups (3/4 pound) roasted nuts.

SOUPS, MAINS & SIDES

SOUPS, MAINS & SIDES

Chicken Lentil Vegetable Soup with Herbes de Provence

A gentle, homey soup, this makes a savory, easy lunch or supper any time of year.

- 2 cups mixed chopped carrots, celery, and onions
- 1 tablespoon olive oil or other vegetable oil
- 1 small peeled and minced garlic clove, optional
- 4 cups commercial chicken broth or vegetable broth, preferably reduced-sodium
- 2/3 cup uncooked red lentils, rinsed and drained
- 1 cup diced unpeeled red bliss or Yukon gold potatoes
- 1 1/2 teaspoons homemade or purchased herbes de provence seasoning (p.76)
- 2 to 3 tablespoons *each* chopped fresh parsley leaves and fresh chives or green onion tops plus more for garnish
- 1 teaspoon *each* chopped fresh thyme leaves and fresh culinary lavender buds, optional
- 1 1/2 to 2 cups cooked diced chicken white meat

  Coarse crystal salt and freshly ground black pepper to taste, optional

Stir together the carrots, celery, and onions and oil in a 4 quart or similar pot. Cook over medium heat, stirring, until the vegetables begin to brown, about 7 minutes. Stir in the garlic (if using); cook 1 minute. Stir in the broth, lentils, potatoes, herbes de provence and 1 cup water and bring the mixture to a gentle boil. Cover and cook, stirring occasionally, for about 20 minutes, until the lentils and potatoes are just tender.

Stir in the fresh parsley, chives, thyme, and lavender (if using), and chicken meat. Taste and add salt and pepper as needed. Cook 3 or 4 minutes until piping hot. Serve garnished with more fresh parsley, chives, thyme, and lavender, as desired. The soup may be covered and refrigerated up to 4 days. Makes 5 or 6 main-dish servings, about 1 1/2 cups each.

SOUPS, MAINS & SIDES

Lacquered Apricot-Lavender Chicken Thighs

This recipe is one in a popular category of Asian-style poultry dishes described as "lacquered," and it's aptly named: The finished chicken pieces boast a crispy skin and distinctive, lacquer-like deep orange sheen that invites you to take a bite! The reward inside is meat that's moist, slightly spicy-sweet, and delightfully savory from the fragrant marinade of apricot, lavender, gingerroot and soy sauce.

- -

3/4	cup *each* apricot preserves and tomato ketchup	1 1/2	teaspoons *each* very finely crushed or minced dried culinary lavender buds and peeled and minced fresh gingerroot
3	tablespoons soy sauce, preferably reduced-sodium	12	medium-sized (5 to 6 ounces each) skin-on chicken thighs, trimmed of excess fat
1	tablespoon Dijon mustard		

Vigorously stir together the preserves, ketchup, soy sauce, mustard, lavender, and gingerroot in a small deep bowl. Set aside about half the marinade for basting. Put the chicken pieces and the remaining marinade in a large, sturdy 1-gallon plastic zip bag. Seal the bag, then shake it until all the pieces are well coated. Refrigerate at least 2 hours or up to 12 hours.

Preheat the oven to 400 degrees F. Generously spray a very large rimmed baking sheet with nonstick spray. Using a slotted spoon or fork and letting the marinade drip off, transfer the chicken thighs to the baking sheet. Space them slightly separated and underside up. Baste them with a generous third of the reserved marinade. Bake them (upper third of oven) for 20 to 25 minutes, or until lightly browned. Turn over the thighs and baste the skins with most of the remaining marinade. Bake for 20 to 25 minutes longer, or until cooked through, glazed and crispy at the edges; watch carefully and lower the heat to 375 degrees F the last 10 minutes if they begin to look charred. Baste with the remaining marinade. Transfer to a heatproof serving dish and serve. The chicken may be stored, covered and refrigerated, for up to 4 days, then reheated, covered, in a medium oven. Makes 12 chicken pieces, 6 generous servings.

SOUPS, MAINS & SIDES

SOUPS, MAINS & SIDES

Country-Style Pork Ribs with Lavender-Spice Barbecue Sauce

Like many roasted dinners, this makes a hearty, easy meal. Round it out as shown with the Winter Vegetable Medley.

- 1 cup commercial tomato-based barbecue sauce
- 2 to 4 tablespoons sweet (not Seville) orange marmalade or apricot preserves, to taste
- 2 finely chopped or grated peeled fresh gingerroot
- 1 1/4 teaspoons *each* ground allspice and finely chopped dried culinary lavender buds
- 2 pounds boneless country-style pork ribs, trimmed and cut apart as needed

  Salt and pepper to taste

  Lavender sprigs for garnish, optional

In a large, deep bowl, stir or whisk together the barbecue sauce, marmalade, gingerroot, allspice, and lavender until very well blended. Remove 1/3 cup of the sauce and set aside for basting. Add the pork pieces to the bowl and stir until coated all over with the sauce. Cover and refrigerate at least 15 minutes and up to 1 hour.

Preheat the oven to 400 degrees F. Arrange the pork pieces and sauce in a non-stick spray–coated roasting pan large enough to hold them without crowding. Roast in the upper third of the oven for 30 minutes. If fat has accumulated in the pan, discard about half of it. Baste the tops of the pieces with all the reserved barbecue sauce. Roast 8 to 10 minutes longer, or until the largest pork pieces are cooked through. Serve in the roasting pan or arrange the pork, sauce-side up, in a serving dish. Serve as is, or with lavender sprigs and roasted vegetables (p. 28) as shown, if desired. Makes 4 to 6 servings.

SOUPS, MAINS & SIDES

SOUPS, MAINS & SIDES

Lavender-Spice Winter Vegetable Medley

This fragrant vegetable medley is a great change of pace from the usual roasted vegetables and will round out almost any dinner. Slip it into the oven while roasting poultry or meat for an easy side. It goes well with the Country-Style Pork Ribs as shown on p. 27 Use whatever winter vegetables you have on hand.

• •

- 1 1/2 tablespoons unsalted butter
- 3/4 teaspoon finely crushed, or minced, or coarsely ground dried culinary lavender buds
- 1/2 teaspoon *each* ground coriander and mild curry powder
- 1/2 teaspoon peeled and minced fresh gingerroot
- 1/2 teaspoon fine sea salt, or more to taste
- 2 tablespoons clover honey or other mild honey
- 6 1/2 to 7 cups assorted winter vegetables, such as peeled baby carrots; unpeeled whole baby gold potatoes or 1-inch cubes unpeeled red bliss potatoes; 3/4-inch cubes peeled sweet potato; and small, trimmed Brussels sprouts

Preheat the oven to 400 degrees F. Combine the butter, lavender, coriander, curry powder, gingerroot, and salt in a 9- by 13-inch (or similar) flat baking dish. Place in the oven and heat until the butter melts and the spices are heated, about 5 minutes. Remove from the oven and very thoroughly stir in the honey and vegetables.

Roast (middle rack), stirring occasionally, for 35 to 45 minutes, or until a large carrot pierced in the thickest part with a fork is tender. Add more salt to taste. Serve immediately, or cover and refrigerate for up to 3 days. Reheat, covered, in a 325 degree oven for about 15 minutes. Makes 4 to 6 side-dish servings.

Lavender Lessons: A member of the large mint family, culinary lavender teams up readily with many of its cousins, including not only mint but thyme, basil, oregano, rosemary, and marjoram. Pair equal parts crushed culinary lavender buds, oregano, and thyme in soups and stews for a pleasing Mediterranean herbal flavor.

SOUPS, MAINS & SIDES

South of France–Style Spicy Fish Stew

I wouldn't call this bouillabaisse or suggest that it's an authentic Provençal stew. But this piquant one-pot meal does capture the spirit and robustness of the classic dish. The stew will be improved with the optional saffron, but is good without it.

3	tablespoons olive oil	3	to 3 1/2 cups canned chicken broth, preferably reduced-sodium
1	cup *each* diced onions, celery, and sweet red or green pepper		Generous pinch finely crumbled or crushed saffron threads, optional
1	teaspoon *each* coarsely ground dried culinary lavender buds and dried thyme leaves	1	14- to 15-ounce can diced tomatoes, including juice
1/2	teaspoon *each* dried oregano leaves and finely crushed fennel seeds	1/3	cup chopped fresh parsley, plus sprigs for garnish
1/4	teaspoon *each* freshly ground black pepper and ground cayenne pepper	1 1/2	pounds boneless, skinless cod, haddock, halibut, sea bass, or other mild, firm white fish fillets, cut into 2-inch chunks
1	large peeled, minced garlic clove		
2	cups peeled, cubed (1/3-inch) thin-skinned boiling potatoes		Fine flake sea salt, to taste

In a large soup pot over medium-high heat, cook the oil, onion, celery, sweet pepper, lavender, thyme, oregano, fennel seeds, black pepper, and cayenne pepper until the onions begin to brown, about 5 minutes. Stir in the garlic and potatoes; cook 1 minute longer.

Add the broth and saffron (if using) to the pot. Bring to a gentle boil; cook, uncovered, 15 to 20 minutes, until the potatoes are tender. Add the tomatoes and parsley; cook 5 minutes longer. Stir in the fish and cook, gently stirring several times, until the pieces are just opaque and cooked through, 3 to 4 minutes. Add salt to taste. Serve piping hot in soup plates. Garnish with parsley. Makes 5 or 6 main dish servings, about 2 cups each.

SOUPS, MAINS & SIDES

Asian-Inspired Baked Ginger-Lavender Salmon Fillets

Part of the lavender-ginger-soy seasoning mixture serves as a marinade, the other, as a simple finishing sauce.

- - -

2	teaspoons *each* minced dried culinary lavender buds and peeled and minced fresh gingerroot
1/2	teaspoon *each* finely grated fresh orange zest and prepared mustard
2	tablespoons *each* olive oil and clover honey or other mild honey
3	tablespoons *each* orange juice and soy sauce, preferably reduced-sodium
4	to 6 5- to 7-ounce portions boneless, skin-on salmon fillets
1/4	teaspoon *each* coarse crystal salt and freshly ground black pepper, or more to taste
	Lemon wedges for garnish

In a flat 9- by 13-inch (or similar) flat baking dish, thoroughly stir together the lavender, gingerroot, orange zest, mustard, olive oil, honey, orange juice, and soy sauce. Remove 3 tablespoons to a microwave-safe cup. Put the fillets in the dish, moistening the tops and laying skin-side down. Cover and marinate for 15 to 30 minutes.

Preheat the oven to 400 degrees F. Bake (upper third) for 5 or 6 minutes. Start checking for desired doneness by cutting into the center of a thick fillet with a paring knife. For rare, cook until only 1 inch around the center is still translucent; for medium, until opaque except for center 1/3 inch; for well-done, until opaque throughout. Set aside, covered with foil, for 5 minutes to finish cooking. Using a slotted spoon, transfer fillets to a platter. Stir the salt and pepper into the reserved marinade, then microwave 30 seconds; stir again and drizzle over the fillets. Garnish with lemon wedges and serve. Makes 4 to 6 main-dish servings.

SOUPS, MAINS & SIDES

SOUPS, MAINS & SIDES

SOUPS, MAINS & SIDES

Seared Fresh Pineapple and Prosciutto Salad

I was surprised when I first teamed up lavender and pineapple—they are made for one another! And both lavender and pineapple go with smoked meats and toasted nuts, as well. If you don't have prosciutto, try substituting a good quality thin-sliced smoked ham.

- -

1/2	tablespoon safflower oil or similar vegetable oil	4	to 6 cups mixed crisp bitter greens, such as escarole, romaine, curly endive, and arugula
3	to 4 ounces prosciutto, trimmed of excess fat and cut into bite-sized pieces		About 1/2 cup lavender white balsamic vinaigrette (p.74)
2	cups fresh 1-inch pineapple chunks or large tidbits		About 1/2 cup cubed or crumbled mild goat cheese, optional
3	tablespoons lavender syrup (p.65) or gourmet lavender-fruit syrup p. (68)		About 1/3 cup chipotle honey-roasted nuts (p. 20)

In a nonstick skillet over high heat, combine the oil and prosciutto and cook, stirring, until it is just frizzled and browned, about 2 minutes. Set the prosciutto aside. In the same skillet, cook the pineapple and syrup, stirring, until the syrup reduces and the pineapple chunks brown, about 3 minutes. Continue to cook, stirring constantly, until the chunks are well seared; watch carefully to prevent burning. Immediately take the skillet off the heat.

Toss the greens lightly with the dressing. Arrange on a serving platter or on 4 to 6 salad plates. Top with the prosciutto, pineapple, goat cheese (if using), and nuts, then drizzle lightly with more dressing. Serve immediately, along with a cruet of dressing if desired. Makes 4 to 6 servings.

SOUPS, MAINS & SIDES

SOUPS, MAINS & SIDES

Fruit Salad with Lavender-Mint Dressing

Lavender enhances almost all fruits, so choose whatever ones you like for this recipe. Although elegant served as shown, for an easy, equally delectable presentation just add the dressing to taste to any fruit bowl or compote.

DRESSING

- 1/3 cup lavender syrup (p. 65), gourmet lavender-fruit syrup (p. 66), or lavender-ginger syrup (p.68)
- 2 teaspoons *each* chopped fresh mint and peeled and minced fresh gingerroot
- 2 to 3 teaspoons strained fresh lemon juice, to taste
- 1/8 teaspoon finely shredded or grated fresh orange zest
- Pinch of sea salt

FRUIT SALAD

- About 4 cups assorted fresh fruits, such as orange, pineapple, melon, peach and mango slices and strawberries, raspberries, blueberries, blackberries and cherries
- Small fresh burrata balls or mozzarella balls or slices, optional
- Small fresh mint leaves and 2 pinches orange zest
- Fresh or dried culinary lavender sprigs or bloomlets for garnish, optional

Whisk together the lavender syrup, mint, gingerroot, lemon juice, orange zest and salt in a small deep bowl. Let stand while the fruits are readied, or refrigerate up to 2 days.

For plated salads arrange the fruits and burrata balls or mozzarella balls attractively on 4 or 5 salad plates. Drizzle each plate with a little dressing. Garnish the plates lightly with mint leaves and orange zest. Add lavender sprigs or bloomlets, if you like. If desired, pass the leftover dressing so diners can add more to taste. For a fruit bowl, omit the burrata. Stir together all the fruit with the mint leaves and orange zest. Stir in 3 to 4 tablespoons dressing to taste and serve immediately. Makes 4 or 5 side-dish servings.

SOUPS, MAINS & SIDES

Fruited Chicken Salad with Lavender-Honey Dressing

Colorful and savory, with a light, creamy, lavender-infused honey dressing, this chicken salad is perfect for serving at a luncheon, supper, or buffet. Diced celery and apples add crunch; dried cranberries lend chew and touches of sweetness; and all mingle to nicely complement the plump chunks of white meat chicken. The dish is ideal for entertaining because it is best made ahead so the flavors can blend.

Additionally, the recipe is gluten-free and mild enough to please those with an aversion to spicy or exotic fare. Double or triple the recipe, if desired.

DRESSING

- 1 1/4 cups mayonnaise, preferably full-fat
- 1 1/2 to 2 tablespoons unflavored rice vinegar, white wine vinegar, or other mild, light-colored vinegar, to taste
- 2 tablespoons clover honey
- 3 tablespoons chopped fresh chives or 1 1/2 tablespoons dried chopped chives
- 1 teaspoon finely minced fresh culinary lavender buds or 3/4 teaspoon finely crushed or coarsely ground dried culinary lavender buds
- 1/4 teaspoon *each* dry mustard powder, sea salt and freshly ground black pepper, or to taste

CHICKEN SALAD

- 3 1/2 to 4 cups coarsely diced (3/4-inch pieces) cooked and cooled chicken breast white meat*
- 1 1/3 cups *each* diced (1/4-inch pieces) celery and diced (1/2-inch pieces) unpeeled sweet-tart apples, preferably red-skinned apples
- 3/4 cup dried sweetened cranberries
- 4 to 6 cups mesclun or other mixed greens

    Red and white Belgian endive leaves, for serving, optional

    Chipotle honey-roasted nuts and lavender bloomlets, for garnish, optional

SOUPS, MAINS & SIDES

(continued)

SOUPS, MAINS & SIDES

For the dressing: In a nonreactive medium bowl, stir together the mayonnaise, vinegar, honey, chives, lavender, mustard, salt, and pepper until well blended. Taste and add a little more vinegar and salt and pepper, as desired. Refrigerate for at least 30 minutes or up to 4 days. Stir well before using.

For the chicken salad: Combine the cooked chicken, celery, apples, and cranberries in a large nonreactive bowl. Add the dressing, tossing until evenly incorporated. Cover and refrigerate so flavors can blend at least 45 minutes or up to 2 days. Taste and add salt and pepper as needed, stirring well. Serve on a bed of greens, garnished with the Belgian endive, nuts, (if using), and fresh lavender buds if desired. Makes four 1 1/2-cup servings.

* If not using previously roasted chicken breast meat, ready the chicken as follows: Trim all fat from 1 1/2 pounds boneless, skinless chicken breast halves. Cut each breast half into 2 or 3 pieces. Place in a medium saucepan and barely cover with chicken broth. Bring to a gentle boil over medium-high heat, then lower the heat so the pot simmers gently. Cover and cook for 12 to 15 minutes, or until the chicken pieces are just cooked through in the center. Test for doneness by cutting into the thickest part of several large pieces; if the meat looks opaque, they are done. Remove from the heat and let cool, then refrigerate covered until needed. Pat the chicken pieces dry with paper towels and cut the meat into 3/4-inch pieces; use as directed in the recipe.

Lavender Lessons: Culinary lavender has lots of spicy, fruity and citrusy flavor notes, so it heightens the appeal of most fruit recipes (especially pear and pineapple), as well as many boldly seasoned dishes like curries and stir-fries. And lavender just loves ginger, cardamom and other "gingerbread" spices, so incorporate it to add extra flavor and aroma to spiced baked good recipes.

DESSERTS & BAKED GOODS

Lavender-Vanilla Cupcakes

These tempting lavender- and vanilla-scented cupcakes have a noticeably tender-soft texture and mellow flavor. Top them with Lavender-Berry Buttercream Frosting (p. 44) —yum!

- -

1 2/3 cups unbleached all-purpose white flour

1 cup lavender sugar (p. 77)

2 teaspoons baking powder

1/4 teaspoon baking soda

Generous 1/8 teaspoon fine table salt

8 tablespoons (1 stick) unsalted butter, cool and firm (not hard) and cut into 1-inch pieces

1/3 cup plain low-fat or regular Greek-style yogurt whisked together with 1/2 cup water

2 large eggs, plus 1 large yolk, at room temperature

2 teaspoons vanilla extract

Place a rack in the middle third of the oven; preheat to 350 degrees F. Line 15 to 18 2 1/4- to 2 1/2-inch (standard-sized) muffin tin cups with paper liners.

Thoroughly stir together the flour, lavender sugar, baking powder, baking soda, and salt in a large mixer bowl. Sprinkle the butter over top. Mix on low speed until the mixture forms very fine crumbs, about 2 minutes.

In a medium bowl, using a whisk or a fork, beat together the yogurt-water, eggs and yolk, and vanilla until very smooth. Gradually pour the egg mixture into the flour mixture, beating on low speed until evenly incorporated. Raise the speed to medium and beat 1 minute; stop and scrape down the bowl as needed.

DESSERTS & BAKED GOODS

(continued)

Divide the batter equally among the cups; using a heaping 1/4-cup measure to form portions works well. Spread the batter out to cup edges. Bake (middle rack) for 17 to 22 minutes, or until puffed on top and a toothpick tested in a center cupcake comes out with moist crumbs; the tops will be only lightly browned.

Cool the cupcakes completely on wire racks. Top with buttercream frosting. The cupcakes are best when fresh but may be stored, airtight, in a cool spot for 24 hours. They may also be frozen, airtight, for up to 1 week. Let them return to room temperature before frosting and serving. Makes 15 to 18 cupcakes.

Lavender-Berry Buttercream Frosting

This frosting is not only pretty and spreads well, but tastes divine. The recipe makes enough to generously frost 18 cupcakes, an 8-inch cake, or a large batch of cookies. I prefer to rely on only natural color to tint this frosting, so incorporate a few berries. Blackberries and blueberries produce the brightest hue, but strawberries and raspberries lend a pleasing shade, too. All will add depth to the lush lavender flavor.

Note that if you are yearning for a more vivid lavender-tinted frosting, you'll need to incorporate some drops of purple food coloring.

• •

- 3 tablespoons chopped fresh or thawed frozen blackberries, raspberries, strawberries, or blueberries
- 2 1/2 teaspoons dried culinary lavender buds
- 1/2 teaspoon finely grated fresh lemon zest (yellow part of the skin)

- 8 tablespoons (1 stick) slightly softened unsalted butter, cut into chunks
- 1 tablespoon fresh lemon juice
- 1/8 teaspoon raspberry extract, optional
- 4 cups powdered sugar, plus more as needed

  Drops purple food coloring, optional

DESSERTS & BAKED GOODS

Combine 3 tablespoons water, the berries, lavender buds, and lemon zest in a 2-cup microwave-safe glass measure or similar-sized bowl. Cover with a microwave cover and microwave on full power for 40 seconds. Using a fork, mash the berries against the cup sides. Microwave on full power 30 to 40 seconds longer, just until the mixture begins to bubble up. Let stand in the microwave to cool and steep for 5 minutes, then stir and set aside until completely cooled.

Stir the liquid through a fine mesh sieve into a large mixer bowl; discard the seeds and buds. Add the butter, lemon juice, and raspberry extract (if using) to the mixer bowl. Beat on low speed 1 minute. Add 1 cup powdered sugar and beat until smoothly incorporated. Scraping down the bowl sides occasionally, repeat until all 4 cups sugar are incorporated. Add the food color, (if using). Beat on medium speed just until the coloring is evenly incorporated and the buttercream has a smooth, spreadable consistency. If it is too dry to spread, thoroughly beat in a little room temperature water until spreadable; if too soft, beat in more powdered sugar. Note that the buttercream will stiffen slightly as it stands.

Use immediately or place in an airtight, nonreactive storage container and refrigerate for up to 4 days. Or freeze, airtight, for up to several weeks. Let the buttercream return to cool room temperature; beat or stir to obtain a smooth, spreadable consistency before using.

To decorate: Using a table knife, swirl on enough frosting on cookie or cupcake tops to yield a 1/4-inch-thick layer, or as desired. Or to pipe the frosting, put it in a pastry bag fitted with an open star tip and pipe as desired. Serve the treats immediately or place in a single layer in an airtight container. Store at cool room temperature for up to 2 days or freeze, airtight, for up to 1 week. Let come to room temperature before serving. Makes enough to frost 18 cupcakes.

DESSERTS & BAKED GOODS

Easy Royal Frosting

Royal frosting delivers the prettiest look when you want to add a smooth top coat and detailed piping to cookies. Many royal frostings require beating, but here the ingredients are simply stirred together. To eliminate the risks of eating uncooked egg whites this recipe calls for commercial meringue powder. Find it with cake decorating supplies in discount department and craft stores or online.

- - -

3 cups powdered sugar (sift after measuring if lumpy)	1/8 teaspoon vanilla, almond, or lavender extract (p.78)
1 tablespoon commercial meringue powder	Assorted food colors, preferably botanical

Thoroughly stir together the sugar, meringue powder, and extract in a large bowl. Gradually and *very thoroughly* stir in 3 to 5 tablespoons water as needed to yield your desired piping or spreading consistency. Divide the icing among several smaller bowls, then tint them whatever colors you like. Keep the icings covered so they don't dry out on top as they stand. They will keep tightly covered and refrigerated for up to 3 days; stir to recombine before using. Or freeze for up to 3 weeks; let them thaw completely and stir well before before using.

DESSERTS & BAKED GOODS

DESSERTS & BAKED GOODS

Lavender Shortbread Fingers or Cut-Out Cookies

Lots of lavender shortbread recipes are in circulation, but few give you the option of creating either eye-catching rolled cut-out cookies or simple shortbread fingers. Whichever you choose, the cookies or fingers will be exceedingly fragrant and buttery. Due to the long, slow baking and the crystal sugar on top, the fingers will also have a noticeably crispy, crunchy texture. The fingers are shown on page 43 and the cut-out cookies on page 47.

- -

1/2	cup granulated sugar		Scant 1/2 teaspoon salt
1	tablespoon dried culinary lavender buds	2	cups unbleached all-purpose white flour
13	tablespoons cool but slightly soft unsalted butter, cut into chunks		About 3 tablespoons purple or clear crystal decorating sugar

1 1/2 teaspoons vanilla extract

To make the dough: Combine the sugar and lavender in a food processor; process for 4 to 5 minutes or until the lavender is very finely ground. In a large bowl, with a mixer on medium speed, beat the butter, sugar-lavender mixture, vanilla, and salt just until evenly blended, scraping down the bowl as needed. On low speed, beat in most of the flour just until the mixture begins to form a mass. If the mixer motor labors, stop and stir in the flour with a large spoon. Sprinkle over the remaining flour, then working in the bowl, knead it in with your hands just until evenly incorporated; don't overmix.

To make shortbread fingers: Line a very large low-rimmed baking sheet with baking parchment. Working on a sheet of parchment, roll out the dough into an evenly thick generous 9- by 12-inch rectangle; if necessary cut and patch it to make the sides fairly even. Even out the dough top by topping it with parchment and lightly rolling

DESSERTS & BAKED GOODS

back and forth. Then flip over the dough (still attached to the sheets) so the smooth underside is up. Peel off the top sheet. Using a large knife, cut away and discard the uneven edges all around. Sprinkle the crystal sugar evenly over the top and pat down lightly all over to embed. Cut the dough crosswise into quarters and then lengthwise into eighths to form 32 fingers. Lift fingers with a spatula and space them slightly apart on the baking sheet. If too soft to handle easily at any point, refrigerate the dough briefly, then continue.

Position a rack in the middle of the oven; preheat to 300 degrees F. Bake (middle rack) for 20 to 25 minutes, or until the fingers are nicely browned all over. Lower the heat to 250 degrees F and bake 15 to 20 minutes longer to further crisp the fingers. Turn off the oven and let them stand in it until completely cooled. Store the shortbread fingers, airtight, at room temperature for up to 10 days; or freeze them for up to 2 months. Thaw at room temperature before serving. Makes 32 shortbread fingers.

To make cut-out shortbreads: Line several large low-rimmed baking sheets with baking parchment. Divide the dough in half. Roll out each 1/4-inch thick between sheets of parchment; be sure the dough is evenly thick all over. Slide the dough and parchment onto a baking sheet, Refrigerate until cold and firm, about 25 minutes. Preheat the oven to 300 degrees F. Working with one chilled dough portion, peel off the top sheet, pat back down into place. Then flip over the dough; peel off second sheet. Cut out the cookies using 2- to 3-inch cutters. Lift from paper with a spatula, spacing 1 1/2-inches apart on sheets. If not planning to ice the cookies, add crystal sugar as desired, lightly pressing down. Bake (middle rack) one pan at a time for 17 to 23 minutes or until lightly tinged. Let firm up on sheets 5 minutes; transfer to racks. Let cool completely. Add royal icing as shown on p. 47, or as desired. Iced shortbreads will keep airtight for up to 1 week; or freeze for up to 2 months. Makes 25 to 40, depending on cutter size.

DESSERTS & BAKED GOODS

Lavender-Vanilla Snowball Cookies

These are the best snowball cookies I've ever made. They have an amazingly tender, melt-in-the-mouth texture and mild yet sublime lavender-vanilla flavor and aroma.

Note that this recipe calls for a length of vanilla bean, not the seeds scraped from a split bean. Even after the seeds are removed, vanilla beans are intensely flavorful, so don't throw them out. To make the vanilla powdered sugar needed here use a bean that is a bit dry or even brittle. (If necessary, let a moist piece of bean stand uncovered to dry out a day or so.) Yes, these cookies are still worth making even if you must skip the vanilla bean, just not quite as amazing.

• •

1 1/4	cups powdered sugar, divided	1	cup (2 sticks) unsalted butter, at room temperature and cut into chunks
2	teaspoons dried culinary lavender buds	2 1/2	teaspoons vanilla extract
1-inch-long	piece dry vanilla bean, finely chopped, optional		Generous 1/8 teaspoon fine table salt
		2	cups plus 2 tablespoons unbleached all-purpose white flour

Position a rack in the middle of the oven; preheat to 350 degrees F. Combine 3/4 cup powdered sugar in a food processor with the lavender buds and vanilla bean bits, if using. Process for 3 to 4 minutes, or until the lavender is ground fairly fine. Stir the processed sugar mixture through a very fine mesh sieve into a deep, medium bowl; discard any lavender and vanilla bits. Very thoroughly stir the remaining 1/2 cup powdered sugar into the processed sugar.

In a large bowl, with a mixer on low, then medium speed, beat the butter, 1/2 cup of the powdered sugar mixture, the vanilla extract, and salt until well blended and smooth. On low speed, gradually beat in the flour just until the mixture begins to mass. If

DESSERTS & BAKED GOODS

(continued)

the mixer motor labors, knead in the last of the flour by hand until fully and evenly incorporated. Shape the dough into a long, evenly- thick log, then cut crosswise into quarters. Cut each quarter into 8 or 9 portions and shape them into balls. Space about 2 inches apart on baking parchment–lined baking sheets. Bake (middle rack) for 12 to 16 minutes, or until the cookies are just barely tinged at the edges.

Let the cookies stand on a cooling rack until cooled completely. Working with 4 or 5 cookies at a time, gently roll them in the remaining powdered sugar mixture until lightly coated all over. Arrange them rounded side up in a flat storage container or on a serving tray. Then put the leftover sugar in a fine sieve and sift it over their tops to create a powdery snow–like look. They will keep covered at room temperature for up to a week. Or freeze airtight for 2 months; thaw completely before serving. Makes 32 to 36 cookies.

DESSERTS & BAKED GOODS

Lavender Thumbprint Cookies

Not only are these eye-catching, but the tender lavender-flavored dough pairs perfectly with almost any seedless preserves or purchased or homemade lemon curd. For a novel touch, ready the cookies with two fillings used together: The pretty thumbprints here contain lemon curd with dabs of apricot preserves on top—a colorful and delish combo!

- - -

- 1 1/2 cups (3 sticks) unsalted butter, at room temperature
- 1 cup homemade lavender sugar (p. 77)
- 2 1/2 teaspoons vanilla extract
- 1 teaspoon freshly grated lemon zest (yellow part of the skin)
- 1/4 teaspoon fine table salt
- 3 large egg yolks, at room temperature
- 3 1/3 cups unbleached all-purpose white flour
- About 2 1/2 tablespoons clear sparkling sugar, sanding sugar or granulated sugar for garnish
- About 1 cup seedless raspberry or apricot preserves or lemon curd, or a combination

In a large bowl with the mixer on medium speed, beat together the butter, lavender sugar, vanilla, lemon zest, and salt until very light and well blended, about 2 minutes. Beat in the egg yolks, one at a time until smoothly incorporated; stop and scrape down the bowl as needed. Gradually beat in the flour to form a smooth, slightly soft dough. If the mixer motor labors, stir in the last flour by hand. Let the dough stand for 15 minutes to firm up slightly.

Preheat the oven to 350 degrees F. Thoroughly spray several large low-rimmed baking sheets with nonstick spray. On a sheet of wax paper, divide the dough into quarters; then divide each into 10 to 12 portions. Roll the portions into smooth balls, lightly dipping their tops in the sparkling sugar. Space them about 1 1/2 inches apart on sheets. With a knuckle or thumb, press a deep indentation into each cookie. If the

(continued)

DESSERTS & BAKED GOODS

DESSERTS & BAKED GOODS

cookie edges break apart, smooth them back into shape again.

One sheet at a time, bake the cookies (middle rack) for 10 minutes. Remove from the oven and add a generous teaspoon of filling or combination of fillings to each indentation. Then bake 9 to 11 minutes, until the cookies are baked through and tinged at the edges. Let stand to cool slightly. Transfer to cooling racks; let stand until thoroughly cooled. Store, airtight, at cool room temperature in a single layer between sheets of wax paper for up to 1 week. Or freeze, airtight, for up to 1 month. Makes 40 to 48 2- to 2 1/4-inch cookies.

DESSERTS & BAKED GOODS

DESSERTS & BAKED GOODS

Cranberry-Pear Lavender-Spice Muffins

Both ginger and lavender bring out the mellow, gently fruity pear taste. The pears keep the muffins moist, and the cranberries give them color and zing. Great for the holidays!

1	cup granulated sugar	1/2	teaspoon fine table salt
2	teaspoons *each* finely chopped dried culinary lavender buds and peeled and minced fresh gingerroot	1/4	teaspoon baking soda
			Generous 1/2 teaspoon *each* ground allspice and ground cinnamon
1 1/2	teaspoons freshly grated lemon zest (yellow part of skin)	1	large egg
		1/3	cup *each* corn oil or canola oil and plain Greek-style yogurt
3/4	cup whole fresh or thawed frozen cranberries	3/4	cup low-fat or whole milk
2	cups unbleached all-purpose white flour	3/4	cup peeled, chopped, and drained just-ripe Bartlett pear (1 largish)
2	teaspoons baking powder		

Preheat oven to 425 degrees F. Spray 12 standard-sized muffin tin cups with nonstick spray. In a food processer, process the sugar and lavender buds until the lavender is finely ground, 4 minutes. Remove 1 tablespoon sugar and set aside for garnishing. Add the gingerroot and lemon zest; process 1 minute. Sprinkle the cranberries over the sugar. Process in on-off pulses until they are chopped medium-fine.

Thoroughly stir together flour, baking powder, salt, soda, allspice, and cinnamon in a large bowl. Thoroughly stir in the cranberry-sugar mixture; reach to the bottom and mix well. In a medium bowl, using a fork, thoroughly beat together the egg, oil, and yogurt. Beat in the milk. Stir the milk mixture and pears into the flour mixture just until the dry ingredients are wet and pears are evenly incorporated; don't overmix. Divide the batter among 12 muffin cups; they will be full. Sprinkle the tops with reserved sugar. Bake for 14 to 18 minutes or until golden brown and springy on top. Cool briefly; run a knife around the cups to remove the muffins. They are best served fresh. Makes 12 standard-sized muffins.

DESSERTS & BAKED GOODS

Lavender Summer Fruit and Berry Crumble

A crumble is a bit like a cobbler, but easier: The buttery crumb topping is just strewn over the fruit. Then the dish is slid into the oven and baked until bubbly and golden. The flavors of the fruit, berries and lavender intermingle beautifully in this recipe. It's one of my favorite summer desserts.

- -

1 1/3	cups lavender sugar (p. 77), divided	1/2	teaspoon baking powder
2	tablespoons cornstarch	1/4	teaspoon fine table salt
2 1/2	cups *each* sliced fully ripe, peeled peaches or nectarines and strawberries	8	tablespoons (1 stick) unsalted butter, melted and cooled slightly
1	cup raspberries		Whipped cream, ice cream, heavy cream, or vanilla yogurt for garnish, optional
1 2/3	cups unbleached all-purpose white flour		Fresh culinary lavender buds for garnish, optional

Place a rack in the middle third of the oven; preheat to 375 degrees F. Thoroughly stir 2/3 cup lavender sugar and the cornstarch together in a large bowl. Stir in the peaches, strawberries, and raspberries until evenly incorporated. Evenly spread out the mixture in a 9- by 13-inch (or similar) flat baking dish.

For the crumble topping, very thoroughly stir together the flour, remaining 2/3 cup lavender sugar, baking powder, and salt in a large bowl. Drizzle the butter over top. Mix with a fork until the butter is evenly incorporated; the mixture will look crumbly-clumpy. Sprinkle the crumble topping evenly over the fruit. Bake (middle rack) for 30 to 40 minutes, or until the top is nicely browned and the fruit is bubbly. Let stand to cool slightly.

Serve immediately, or store, refrigerated, for up to 24 hours. (It will lose its crispness if stored longer.) Let return to room temperature or rewarm before serving. Add whipped cream, ice cream, cream, or yogurt, if desired. Garnish with lavender bloomlets (room-temperature servings only), if desired. Makes 5 or 6 servings.

DESSERTS & BAKED GOODS

DESSERTS & BAKED GOODS

Lavender-Lemon Sour Cream Pound Cake

A large, classic lavender-scented pound cake, this always wins raves. If you wish, the batter can be baked in two 5- by 9-inch loaf pans to yield two loaf cakes; reduce baking time to 55-70 minutes.

3	cups unbleached all-purpose white flour plus extra for dusting	6	large eggs, at room temperature
1/4	teaspoon baking soda	1/2	cup sour cream or light sour cream
	Generous 1/2 teaspoon fine table salt	1	tablespoon vanilla extract
1 1/2	cups (3 sticks) unsalted butter, slightly softened	1	tablespoon finely grated lemon zest (yellow part of skin)
3	cups lavender sugar (p. 77)	1/2	teaspoon lavender extract (p. 78), optional

Preheat the oven to 350 degrees F. Generously and evenly spray a large (15-cup or similar) Bundt pan or plain tube pan with nonstick spray. Evenly dust the entire interior with flour, then tap out excess. Sift together the flour, baking soda, and salt onto wax paper. In a large mixer bowl with the mixer on medium speed, beat the butter and lavender sugar until lightened and fluffy, about 2 minutes; occasionally scrape down bowl. Reduce the speed to low and gradually beat in the flour mixture. If the motor labors, stir in the last flour by hand. Add the eggs, one at a time, beating 10 seconds after each. Add the sour cream, vanilla, and zest. Beat on medium speed for 2 minutes, occasionally scraping down sides. Put the batter into the pan, smoothing out the surface.

Bake (middle rack) for 1 hour and 15 to 25 minutes or until the top is nicely browned and a toothpick inserted in the thickest part comes out with a few crumbs clinging. Let the cake cool on a rack for 1 hour. Run a table knife carefully around the pan flutes

DESSERTS & BAKED GOODS

(continued)

DESSERTS & BAKED GOODS

or sides, center tube and under bottom to loosen the cake. When fully loosened, slide it out onto a cake plate. Add optional glaze, if desired. May be frozen, airtight, for up to 3 weeks. Makes about 12 to 14 servings.

Lavender-Lemon Glaze

This glaze can dress up not only pound cake, but cupcakes, cookies and quick breads. If you use bright blue or purple lavender buds the glaze will be pink. Pale-colored buds will lend a creamy hue. The recipe yields enough to drizzle decoratively over the pound cake; double the recipe if you wish to generously glaze the cake all over.

TIP: To give the glaze a brighter color, add a teaspoon or two of blueberries, or a couple black-skinned grapes when you microwave the lavender buds. Very easy, and the result will be a pretty, all-natural shade.

• •

2	teaspoons dried culinary lavender buds	1	tablespoon strained fresh lemon juice
	Grated zest of half a medium-sized lemon	1/8	teaspoon lavender extract (p. 78), optional
1	cup powdered sugar, plus more if needed		

Combine 2 1/2 tablespoons water, the lavender buds and lemon zest in a small, deep microwave-safe bowl. Cover and microwave on full power for 1 minute. Let stand in the microwave to infuse at least 5 and preferably 10 minutes. Stir the liquid through a fine mesh sieve into a deep, medium bowl, pressing down to extract as much lavender-lemon water as possible.

Vigorously stir the powdered sugar, lemon juice and extract (if using) into the lavender-lemon water to obtain a smooth drizzling consistency. Stir in more sugar if the glaze is too thin, or a little water if it is too thick. Drizzle the glaze over the cooled cake, or spoon it over and immediately spread with a knife. Let stand for at least 10 minutes before serving.

Lavender Lesson: To quickly extract the full-bodied natural flavor from culinary lavender, combine 1 to 2 teaspoons dried buds with 1/4 cup water in a large microwave-safe measuring cup. Microwave for 1 minute on high power, then let stand in the microwave to steep for 5 to 15 minutes. Strain the lavender water through a fine mesh sieve; discard the buds. Lavender water can enhance all kinds of beverages from lemonade and ginger ale to smoothies and cocktails.

PANTRY & REFRIGERATOR STAPLES

PANTRY & REFRIGERATOR STAPLES

Lavender Syrup

Culinary lavender has a complex spicy-herbal-floral flavor that enlivens all kinds of dishes, from barbecue sauces, curries, Asian-style fare, and smoked meats to fruit recipes like sundaes, compotes, fruit salads, and bowls of berries, melons, stone fruits, or pineapple. And do try adding a splash of syrup to lemon, lime, peach, apple, and pomegranate beverages. The recipe can be doubled if desired.

If your lavender buds are a bright blue or purple, the syrup will likely have a faint amber or pink tinge. You can bring up the color (as shown here) simply by adding lemon juice. (Its acid reacts with and brightens the natural plant color pigments called anthocyanins.) Pale-colored culinary buds won't contribute much color to syrups, but they pack the same flavor punch.

• •

- 2 cups granulated sugar
- 2 to 2 1/2 tablespoons dried culinary lavender buds, to taste
- 1 teaspoon fresh lemon juice, optional

Stir together 2 cups water and the sugar in a medium-sized nonreactive saucepan over medium heat. Bring to a boil, stirring, then adjust the heat so the mixture boils gently. Cook, stirring occasionally, for 4 minutes to thoroughly dissolve the sugar. Stir in the lavender buds; mash them against the pan sides to bruise them a bit. Let the mixture just return to a boil, then remove from the heat and let stand, covered, so the lavender can fully infuse the syrup, at least 45 minutes or up to 4 hours for fullest flavor. Stir in the lemon juice, if using. Strain the syrup through a fine mesh sieve into a measure. Press down firmly to force through all the liquid. Rinse out the saucepan and return the syrup to it. Bring to a boil and boil for 1 1/2 minutes. Let cool slightly, then put in a bottle or jar (preferably sterilized) and refrigerate. It will keep refrigerated for 2 to 3 months. Makes a generous 2 cups syrup.

PANTRY & REFRIGERATOR STAPLES

Gourmet Lavender-Fruit Syrup

Make this easy, versatile syrup in several lush berry and fruit flavors and keep them at the ready in the refrigerator. Then slosh a tablespoon or two over fruit salad or ice cream, or swirl into yogurt, sodas, sparkling wine, marinades, salad dressings, simple icings, and more.

A whole array of fruits can be used, and each will contribute its own striking color, aroma, and flavor to the finished recipe. The eye-catching syrup shown with the smoothie, page 14 features plums—which pair especially well with lavender.

- -

2 cups granulated sugar	2 tablespoons dried culinary lavender buds
1/2 to 2/3 cup chopped fresh blackberries, raspberries, strawberries, blueberries, cranberries, cherries, pineapple, or pitted, chopped (unpeeled) ripe peaches, nectarines, plums, or apricots	1 tablespoon fresh lemon juice

Stir together 2 cups water, the sugar, and fruit in a medium, nonreactive saucepan over medium heat. Bring to a boil, stirring, then boil gently, stirring occasionally, for 7 to 10 minutes or until the fruit is soft and breaking down. Stir in the lavender buds and lemon juice.

Set aside, covered, and let steep at least 45 minutes, or up to 4 hours for fullest flavor. Strain the syrup through a fine mesh sieve; press down to push through as much liquid as possible. Rinse out the saucepan; add sieved syrup and bring it back to boil. Boil for 1 minute. Cool slightly. Pour into a very clean (preferably sterilized) storage jar or bottle. Store, airtight and refrigerated, 2 to 3 months. Makes a generous 2 cups.

PANTRY & REFRIGERATOR STAPLES

PANTRY & REFRIGERATOR STAPLES

Lavender-Ginger Syrup

If you have never made a lavender syrup, I urge you to finally take the few minutes required and prepare this one now! Even if you make lavender syrups often, do try **this particular one** for perhaps **the best version** you have ever tasted! This one has an ethereal, harmonizing yet simple blending of culinary lavender, fresh gingerroot, and hint of lemon. Lavender has an affinity for many ingredients, and here the intermingling of the herb, spice, and citrus flavors is truly exceptional. (For the syrup color shown, you will need to add in the blueberries.)

How can you use this elixir? Add a splash of it to orange juice, apple juice, or pomegranate juice, or to any fruit-flavored yogurt, smoothie, or fresh fruit dish for a lush yet easy taste boost. Go in a savory direction by adding a tablespoon or two of this syrup to vinaigrettes, pork, duck, ham and other smoked meat pan sauces, or to boost the appeal of almost any Asian-inspired dish.

- - -

2	cups granulated sugar	4	to 5 2-inch-long strips lemon peel (yellow part of skin only), from 1 well-washed lemon
	Enough peeled and thinly sliced well-washed fresh gingerroot pieces, to yield 3/4 cup		
		1/4	cup dried culinary lavender buds
1	tablespoon blueberries (for color), optional	1	tablespoon fresh lemon juice

Combine 2 cups water, the sugar, the ginger slices, blueberries (if using) and lemon peel strips in a 2-quart or similar nonreactive saucepan. Bring to a boil over medium heat, stirring, then adjust the heat so the mixture boils gently. Boil gently, stirring occasionally, for 10 minutes. Remove from the heat and stir in the lavender buds. Let stand to steep at least 30 minutes, or up to 1 hour for more intense flavor.

Strain the steeped syrup through a very fine sieve into a large cup. Press down firmly to extract as much flavor as possible from the solids, then discard them. For a clearer syrup, line the sieve with a slightly dampened double- thickness of cheesecloth before

PANTRY & REFRIGERATOR STAPLES

straining. Rinse out the saucepan and return the syrup to it. Strain the lemon juice through the sieve into the saucepan. Bring the syrup to a boil. Boil for 2 minutes. Let cool and put the syrup in a clean (preferably sterilized) bottle or jar with a nonreactive cap or lid. Refrigerate for up to 3 months. Or freeze, airtight, for up to 6 months. Makes about 2 cups syrup.

PANTRY & REFRIGERATOR STAPLES

PANTRY & REFRIGERATOR STAPLES

5-Minute Lavender-Fruit Preserves

I love preparing lavender-enhanced jams and preserves; this beautiful herb just makes so many fruit flavors sing. But since homemade preserves do take a bit of time, I've came up with a quick, shortcut way to keep an assortment of lush, custom-created lavender preserves on hand. I just buy jams and preserves in favorite flavors and cook them together with ground culinary lavender buds for a few minutes. Then I put them back in the jar and stash in the fridge. In a day or two, the lavender has permeated, and the preserves are ready to enjoy. Stick with preserves, marmalades, and jams for this recipe, as jellies sometimes get runny when recooked.

As for what preserves to use, nearly all I've tried have been good: Raspberry, blackberry, blueberry, plum, apricot, peach, and pineapple are all winners, and lavender-pear preserves are out of this world. Orange, lemon, and other citrus marmalades work well, too. The photograph shows raspberry preserves (far back, right), orange marmalade in the forefront and back, left, and my unique combo flavor of pear-lemon marmalade with some seedless raspberry preserves in the middle.

• •

1 10- to 12-ounce purchased jar preserves, jam, or marmalade	1 to 2 teaspoons ground or finely chopped dried culinary lavender buds, to taste

Combine the preserves and lavender in a nonreactive medium saucepan over medium heat. Bring almost to a boil, stirring, then reduce the heat and gently simmer for 5 minutes. Let stand until cooled, then put the preserves back in their jar, or any storage jar desired. Keep the preserves refrigerated.

PANTRY & REFRIGERATOR STAPLES

Lavender-Infused Balsamic Vinegar or White Balsamic Vinegar

It's fun, inexpensive, and a gourmet treat to make your own lavender-infused balsamic vinegar. The herb's complex fruity and floral notes intermingle beautifully with the deep, sweet-and-sour elements of the grape-based vinegar. The pairing is a natural!

Actually, balsamic vinegar and white balsamic vinegar are different products. But they are infused with lavender in exactly the same way: Just tuck some lavender sprigs or buds into the bottle and in about a week you have lavender-infused vinegar ready to use.

Aged balsamic vinegar features the cooked juice of late-harvested Lambrusco or Trebbiano white grapes gradually reduced into a thick, dark syrup. Because it's so intense, just drizzle a few drops over figs, berries, plums, creamy cheeses, and panna cottas for a ping of deeply satisfying flavor.

White balsamic vinegar is usually a white wine vinegar that has been enlivened with the freshly pressed juices, or must, of sweet grapes. White balsamic vinegar is not generally thick or concentrated, and can be used like most vinegars in salad dressings and sauces. It's delightful in the vinaigrette recipe on page 74.

• •

10 to 12 sprigs (bloom heads) fresh or dried culinary lavender or 2 to 3 teaspoons dried culinary lavender buds

About 1/2 cup aged balsamic vinegar or white balsamic vinegar, or as needed

If using lavender sprigs, trim off the stems so the sprigs fit the bottle or jar used. Tuck them into the bottle, then add enough vinegar to cover; push them down if necessary. If using buds, just add to the bottle of vinegar, close, and shake well. Let stand at least a week before using. Leave the lavender sprigs or buds in the bottle

PANTRY & REFRIGERATOR STAPLES

and occasionally top it off with more vinegar. Or if preferred, remove and discard the lavender after 2 or 3 weeks.

Be sure to use a nonreactive stopper or lid to prevent corrosion. Store in a dark, cool place for up to 1 year. Makes about 1/2 cup infused vinegar.

PANTRY & REFRIGERATOR STAPLES

Lavender–White Balsamic Vinaigrette

You'll need some lavender-infused white balsamic vinegar on hand to create this tempting vinaigrette. Infusing your own vinegar (p. 72) to use is super-quick and easy, and your product will be much better and cheaper than store-bought.

Due to the rich, fruity notes of both white balsamic vinegar and culinary lavender, this dressing goes well with many of the popular goat cheese, fruit, and toasted nut salads. It's delightful topping a fresh fig salad plate, as shown, and is equally good over a bed of greens, walnuts, and sliced peaches, or perhaps pears, dried cranberries, and bacon bits. Be sure to use a lavender-infused *white balsamic vinegar* or Italian *sweet white wine vinegar* as the base for this dressing. These are usually golden or tawny colored, fluid, and slightly sweet, and are *not* aged.

- 1/2 to 1 tablespoon clover honey, or to taste
- 1/4 cup homemade or purchased lavender-infused white balsamic vinegar
- 1/2 teaspoon *each* prepared mustard, preferably Dijon-style, and yellow mustard seeds
- 1/4 teaspoon *each* fine sea salt and coarsely ground black pepper, plus more to taste
- 1/4 to 1/2 teaspoon finely crushed or minced culinary lavender buds, optional
- 1/2 cup extra-virgin olive oil

In a 2-cup measure or similar-sized deep bowl, thoroughly whisk together the honey, vinegar, mustard, mustard seeds, salt, pepper, and lavender buds (if using) until the prepared mustard is smoothly incorporated. Slowly pour in the olive oil, whisking constantly until thickened and smoothly incorporated. Taste and add more honey, salt, and pepper as needed. Serve the vinaigrette in a cruet that can be shaken or a decorative container that can be whisked. Whisk or shake the dressing to recombine just before dressing a salad. The dressing will keep at room temperature for up to 1 week. Makes a generous 3/4 cup dressing.

PANTRY & REFRIGERATOR STAPLES

PANTRY & REFRIGERATOR STAPLES

Herbes de Provence

This popular, very versatile, aromatic blend can season all sorts of dishes: Combine it with a little oil and lemon juice and rub it into chicken, turkey, pork, or lamb before roasting or sautéing.

Or try this **Herbed Quick Dip** recipe: Vigorously stir 1 teaspoon Herbes de Provence together with an 8-ounce package room-temperature cream cheese and 2 tablespoons finely chopped fresh chives. Almost instantly you've got a lively, savory vegetarian dip or spread for celery sticks or crackers. (Actually, it's best to wait a few minutes before serving so the herbal flavors can mingle a bit.)

TIP: Usually a food processor won't grind up fennel seeds; the blade is too thick, and they just spin round. So they must be crushed before going into the processor. If you don't have a mortar and pestle to do the job, put the seeds between two plastic mats and pound them with the back of a heavy spoon or a kitchen mallet. Or put them on a cutting board, cover with a heavy plastic bag, and firmly roll back and forth or pound with a rolling pin until crushed.

- 1 1/2 tablespoons *each* dried culinary lavender buds and dried rosemary leaves
- 1 tablespoon fennel seeds, crushed
- 1 tablespoon plus 1 teaspoon *each* dried marjoram leaves and dried thyme leaves
- 1 tablespoon *each* dried oregano leaves and dried tarragon leaves

Grind the lavender, rosemary, and crushed fennel seeds in a food processor for 4 to 5 minutes, or until fairly finely ground. Add the marjoram, thyme, oregano, and tarragon and process until well combined, about 1 minute longer. Store in an airtight bottle or jar. Best used within 1 year. Makes about 1/2 cup Herbes de Provence.

PANTRY & REFRIGERATOR STAPLES

Lavender Sugar,
Lavender-Vanilla Sugar, or Lavender Powdered Sugar

Lavender sugar is so handy I try to always keep it in my pantry. Here are just a few easy, tasty uses: Sprinkle it on sliced fruit, berries, or grapefruit halves. Stir it into citrus-flavored orange pekoe or peppermint tea. Use it to replace regular granulated sugar to deepen flavor in pound cakes, brownies, muffins, and other baked goods. Mix it with cinnamon for an exceptional cinnamon toast topping.

TIP: It's easy to double this recipe, but once lavender buds are pulverized, their heady volatile oils begin to fade away. So plan to use the sugar within a couple months.

• •

2 cups granulated sugar, divided   2 tablespoons dried culinary lavender buds

In a food processor or spice grinder grind 1/2 cup sugar and the lavender until very fine (4 to 5 minutes in a processor, 1 minute in a spice grinder). Stir the ground sugar though a very fine mesh sieve, discarding the lavender bits (or save them for another use). Thoroughly stir the sieved sugar into the remaining 1 1/2 cups sugar until evenly incorporated. Or briefly grind the two together in a processor until blended. Store airtight in a cool spot for up to 3 months. Makes 2 cups lavender sugar.

Variation: **Lavender-Vanilla Sugar**-Prepare exactly as directed above, except chop a 1-inch-long piece of completely dry vanilla bean into small bits. Add it with the lavender to the processor. Don't use a soft or moist piece of bean, as it will cause the sugar to clump. Once the mixture is ground, sieve out the lavender and vanilla bean bits and proceed exactly as directed.

Variation: **Lavender Powdered Sugar**-Prepare exactly as directed above except use powdered sugar in place of granulated sugar. Use lavender powdered sugar to garnish desserts, add a coating to cookies, or to sweeten whipped cream. Don't substitute lavender powdered sugar for an equal amount of lavender granulated sugar; the powdered is only about half as dense and much less sweet.

PANTRY & REFRIGERATOR STAPLES

Lavender Extract

I urge you to make your own lavender extract. It's a snap; it's very economical; and it will be much tastier than store-bought. You will need a 2- to 4-ounce glass bottle that has a tight-fitting glass, cork, or plastic top; the alcohol can corrode a metal lid. Use the extract in any baked good you like.

TIP: If you use a vodka, the extract will be a brown color; if you use grain alcohol, it will be clear, due to the extra bleaching action of the higher proof alcohol.

Enough fresh or dried culinary lavender sprigs to fill a 2- to 4-ounce (or similar) glass bottle

Enough neutral-flavored vodka or 190 proof grain alcohol to fill the bottle used

Rinse, then pat the lavender dry. Trim off the stems as needed to fit the bottle. Stuff it full of lavender sprigs; use a fondue fork or skewer if the neck is narrow. Fill the jar to within 1/2 -inch of the top with the vodka or grain alcohol; be sure to submerge the lavender. Let the extract stand 1 week before using. If desired, leave the lavender in the bottle to steep, topping off the alcohol as needed.

For fullest flavor, use it within 1 year. Makes 2 to 4 ounces of extract, depending on the bottle used. Alternatively, strain the extract through a fine mesh sieve, discard the lavender, and return the extract to the bottle. Then add a new lavender sprig or two for a gourmet look.

Index

BEVERAGES & SNACKS

Easy Lavender Pink Lemonade 9
Microwave Mug of Lavender
  Hot Chocolate 10
Lavender-Spice Mulled Apple Cider 13
Lavender Peach Berry Smoothie 15
Lavender-Apple Spice Tea 16
Lavender Pineapple-Orange Mimosas
  (or Mocktails) for a Crowd 19
Chipotle Honey-Roasted Nuts with
  Lavender and Rosemary 20

SOUPS, MAINS & SIDES

Chicken Lentil Vegetable Soup
  with Herbes de Provence 23
Lacquered Apricot-Lavender
  Chicken Thighs 24
Country-Style Pork Ribs with
  Lavender-Spice Barbecue Sauce 26
Lavender-Spice Winter
  Vegetable Medley 28
South of France–Style
  Spicy Fish Stew 31
Asian-Inspired Baked Ginger-Lavender
  Salmon Fillets 32
Seared Fresh Pineapple
  and Prosciutto Salad 35
Fruit Salad with
  Lavender-Mint Dressing 37
Fruited Chicken Salad with
  Lavender-Honey Dressing 38

DESSERTS & BAKED GOODS

Lavender-Vanilla Cupcakes 42
Lavender-Berry Buttercream
  Frosting 44
Easy Royal Frosting 46
Lavender Shortbread Fingers
  or Cut-Out Cookies 48
Lavender-Vanilla Snowball Cookies 50
Lavender Thumbprint Cookies 53
Cranberry-Pear Lavender-Spice
  Muffins 57
Lavender Summer Fruit
  and Berry Crumble 58
Lavender-Lemon Sour Cream
  Pound Cake 60
Lavender-Lemon Glaze 62

PANTRY & REFRIGERATOR STAPLES

Lavender Syrup 65
Gourmet Lavender-Fruit Syrup 66
Lavender-Ginger Syrup 68
5-Minute Lavender-Fruit Preserves 71
Lavender-Infused Balsamic Vinegar
  or White Balsamic Vinegar 72
Lavender–White Balsamic
  Vinaigrette 74
Herbes de Provence 76
Lavender Sugar, Lavender-Vanilla Sugar,
  or Lavender Powdered Sugar) 77
Lavender Extract 78